I SPY with my little eye, something beginning with...

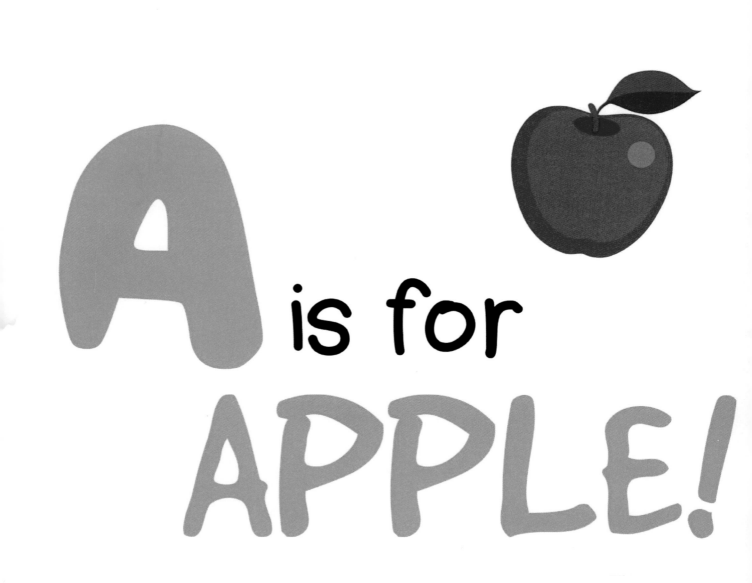

A is for APPLE!

I SPY with my little eye, something beginning with...

B is for BABY!

I SPY with my little eye, something beginning with...

C is for CAKE!

I SPY with my little eye, something beginning with...

D and E

D is for DINOSAUR!

E is for EAR!

I SPY with my little eye, something beginning with...

F **is for** FEATHER!

I SPY with my little eye, something beginning with...

G is for GRASS!

I SPY with my little eye, something beginning with...

H is for HEN!

I SPY with my little eye, something beginning with...

and

i is for  ICE CUBE!

J is for JAM JAR!

I SPY with my little eye, something beginning with...

 K

is for

I SPY with my little eye, something beginning with...

L is for LAMP!

I SPY with my little eye, something beginning with...

M is for MONSTER!

I SPY with my little eye, something beginning with...

N
is for
NINJA!

I SPY with my little eye, something beginning with...

O is for oRANGE!

I SPY with my little eye, something beginning with...

P and Q

P is for **PANDA!**

Q is for **QUEEN!**

I SPY with my little eye, something beginning with...

R

is for

ROCKET!

I SPY with my little eye, something beginning with...

S is for

SNAKE!

I SPY with my little eye, something beginning with...

T is for TOASTER!

I SPY with my little eye, something beginning with...

U and V

U is for UNICoRN!

V is for VASE!

I SPY with my little eye, something beginning with...

W

is for

WINDOW!

I SPY with my little eye, something beginning with...

X is for

XYLOPHONE!

Y is for YO-YO!

Z is for ZEBRA!

THE END!

© 2018 Webber Books

Images and vectors by;

freepix, alekksall, art.shcherbyna, agnessz_arts, anggar3ind, Alliesinteractive, Balasoui, Bakar015, Bimbimkha, brgfx, cornecoba, creativepack, ddraw, dooder, drawnhy97, elsystudio, Emily_b, flaticon, freshgraphix, gordoba, graphicrepublic, iconicbestiary, ibrandify, Jannoon028, johndory, Kamimiart, kat_branch, kbibibi, Kjpargeter, Kraphix, layerace, lesyaskripak, lexamer, lyolya_profitrolya, Macrovector, Makyzz, milano83, Miguel_ruiz, nenilkime, natalka_dmitrova, natkacheva, omegapics, rawpixel, Rayzong, renata.s, , rocketpixel, RosaPuchalt, sketchepedia, stephanie2212, SilviaNatalia, Terdpongvector, titusurya, vectorpocket, Vectortwins, Vector4free, vectorportal, vectorpouch, vecteezy, VVstudio, zirconicusso

Made in the USA
Coppell, TX
20 October 2019